IF ONLY YOU COULD HAVE MISSED ME

Paris, France
January 2018

Graphic design by Julien Gargot from *g.u.i.*, http://g-u-i.net.
Layout is made with the open source software Scribus.
Texts are composed with open source fonts by
Eben Sorkin, https://github.com/EbenSorkin/.
Titles with Merriweather Sans,
body with Merriweather.

Fabienne Brun

IF ONLY YOU COULD HAVE MISSED ME

Translate from french by Imogen Freason

I dedicate this book to my adored sister Pascale, whom I admire and for whom I have the greatest respect. It is hard to rebuild oneself after the age of 50 when your whole existence hangs on a lie. To my little sister Alexandra, whom I love deeply and who, spared from the lies, but living in doubt goes through life like a tight-rope walker in a nebula. To my beautiful children, so that the abstract becomes concrete and to make it easier to one day tell your children, "the strange history of their grandmother". To my American family, who opened their hearts and accepted me without exceptions, who wished to know more about my life and made me want to write it all down.

A big thank you also to:
Mickaël and Pierre, for their precious tips and the time they gave to help me. Miche, Greg's grandmother, who took the time to proof read my writing and correct my mistakes. Imogen, for her suggestions and the English translation. Val, my best friend, for proof reading the English translation. Julien, my nephew, for the cover and the printing.

And last but not least thank you to you Greg, my love, without whom none of this would have been possible. Your cusiosity, your willingness and your optimism allowed this story to see the light of day. Thank you for helping me to find all the little stars who allowed me to reach out and finally meet my Dad.

Fabienne Brun

PREFACE

When I met you Abie, I met a lioness. You are strong and ready to devour life. But you are also a beautiful little bird, delicate and injured by life. Firstly, I wanted to understand you and try to comprehend why you were hurting. When you told me your story, it felt like history was repeating itself. Yes, my uncle's wife told a similar story of her childhood.

Secondly, I knew I wanted to spend my life with you and wanted to take on the challenge of helping you to find some answers to your questions.

And finally, I felt proud. Thanks to you I have been able to accomplish the childhood dream of many children of having an American Uncle, and even outdone this with a whole American family!

One day, like many people around us, I felt that you should

put pen to paper and tell your story. You did it! Congratulations and thank you my love for making me a hero in your life.

Leading this search by your side around the world has been, for the both of us, a wonderful experience and an incredible life project, full of emotional meetings (and there are no doubt many more to come!). We will also have shared this story with your two baby birds, and thanks to us they will now know where they come from and who their family is.

Grég

9/11

I see you standing on a smoking, stinking pile of debris, engulfed in toxic gases, searching for the living and the dead. Bodies and limbs lie all around you. You pick your way as best you can through what is left of the twin towers, crumbled and broken, fallen from their 110 floors in central Manhattan. The thick smoke stings your eyes and nose, chokes you and makes you retch. Six years later this smoke will cost you your life. All around you screams of desperation fill the air. You see people wandering aimlessly, not knowing who they are or where they are going, attempting to escape this war zone. This is the deadly result of the catastrophic events of 11th September 2001, a day that will mark our hearts and souls forever.

I get home from work, and as usual to counter the loneliness, I switch on the television. I see Manhattan island in the sun, a bright blue sky, two majestic towers dominating the horizon, but one is engulfed in flames. Huge plumes of black smoke escape the upper floors of the North Tower of the *World Trade Centre*. Suddenly a passenger aircraft appears to the right of the screen and hits the South tower three quarters of the way up, piercing it right through. After the explosion I see chunks of plane and tower flying in all directions. In the streets there are scenes of panic, I can't see clearly as the hand-held camera is shaking so much. Despite the poor sound quality I can make out the noise of the sirens approaching and the cries of "Oh my god!" over and over again. People are running, crying, crouching to protect themselves, murmuring incomprehensibly. The security forces are shouting "Quick! QUICK!". The police and firefighters attempt to evacuate as fast as possible. I see billowing smoke and bodies plummeting from the upper floors, jumping to avoid being burned alive. I can't bear it... A shiver runs up my spine, my blood goes cold, I feel sick. It reminds me of a disaster movie, and I have to remind myself that this is no poor quality entertainment. I am shocked. When the towers collapse, everyone is stupefied. There is an interminable, deep roar and a huge cloud of dust and ash rises and covers Manhattan within minutes. People are running to escape the debris and the smoke. The cameras show continuous scenes of horror. A man with a bloodied head is talking to a journalist about his narrow escape with his friend. Men and women are helped away, supported by strangers. Everyone looks the same.

Skin colour is no longer a distinguishing feature, just a never-ending grey and I can't tell if it's from the ash or the horror. I sit down on the sofa facing the screen, my whole body awake. My stomach hurts, I feel cold, I feel the tears streaming down my face... I'm scared. Sadness, anger, and sorrow invade me. I feel so powerless. How could someone do this to your home Daddy?

It is the only time I can think of when our paths felt connected, Dad. We were so close, yet so far apart. I wonder what was happening in your head, aside from your response as a professional in an emergency, are you wondering what has happened, or do you already know? What are your first thoughts when confronted with such an immense tragedy? Are you thinking of your loved ones? Where are they now? What are they going through?

I have known about your existence since I was tiny. I have never met you, but I have seen photographs, and when my mother or my auntie told me "he is handsome, funny, charming..." I believed them without hesitation. My mind would travel and I could see myself in the arms of my unknown Daddy. If I had been a boy, I would have been named Patrick, because you loved this name, the name of my uncle's son. I have always been envious of my sister, Pascale, who was photographed in your arms on several occasions. I know she doesn't remember, but I wish I had photographs of you and me. Your absence haunted me throughout my childhood,

my adolescence, and, even now, I miss you. If only you could have missed me...
I always knew that I wanted to find you. I needed to know! According to my mother, she was pregnant with me when you left for the States and she couldn't follow you because of the pregnancy. Is this why she never loved me? Did she resent me for keeping her from you? She never showed me any affection and when she was angry it hurt as much physically as mentally. I never wanted for anything, except the love of my parents.

I compensated for that with food and god knows the hole was a big one to fill. The bulimia set in after the birth of my children. I had lost touch with my mother years before. She didn't even come to my wedding even though I could have done with a parent by my side at that time. This invisible enemy marred a number of years of my existence but I fought back, I went to therapy on my own and with a group. I went to see a nutritionist for two years. I saw shrinks and healers and eventually things got better.
It's tough when you feel alone in a big family. I am one of five children who share a mother. Four girls and a boy. I was the rebel, the one who talked back to my mother or anyone else for that matter, the one who was never happy and always had something to say about everything. I was the one who was afraid of nothing and no one but herself. I didn't shy away from violence when the little ball of anger inside me became unbea-

rable and I thought that everything could be solved with aggressivity. The only person I softened with was my auntie. I worked alongside her in her hair salon every weekend to earn my pocket money. I liked being there, washing hair, mixing colours, listening to the local gossip and hearing women talk about their joys and their pain.

I knew my aunt loved me. She didn't judge me but she didn't let me get away with my bad behaviour. She spoilt me often. I felt like her daughter, and when she would go and play cards on Saturday nights with her husband, it was a pleasure to look after her daughter, my cousin Maud, who is ten years younger. I wanted to get out of my house so badly that when I was 16 I wanted to join the army and if I had been old enough I would have signed immediately. I would have done anything to be independent.

As soon as I turned 18, in 1983, I moved to Paris, where I worked in a restaurant for a year. It was a bit of a struggle, with passing acquaintances and an apartment that looked like a squat. Then I moved to Annemasse, near the Swiss border where I stayed in the hospitality business. It was easy to find jobs in that sector, and I spent a year living with an amazing girl named Patricia. I loved her and her daughter, but when she met the love of her life and fell pregnant again there was no reason for me to stay... I also met a man who took me to live in Auch because it was his home region. I worked in a high school as a secretary but that didn't last long because I didn't love him and I couldn't stop myself from going back to Saint-Etienne. I moved "home", not to live with my mother but with my sister Pascale. I had moved from city to city and found nowhere to settle down, despite the many wonderful people I met on the way. The only relationship that stuck was the one I had with loneliness. Despite my roots in Saint-Etienne I couldn't help but feel like I was like a ship without an anchor, drifting from city to city without really finding what I was looking for.

I have always had a difficult relationship with my mother. We lived and saw too many things that we shouldn't have. Can you make someone love you? It was when I realised that I couldn't that I became bulimic. I couldn't understand how this woman who had carried me in her womb for nine months and given me life, could refuse to give me a name because I wasn't the boy she longed for. She raised me, but she never loved me. It took me a long time to accept this, but now I understand what she lived through, including the pain she felt when you went back to America.

OUR FOSTER FAMILY IN NANCY

When you returned to the USA at the end of 1964, you didn't want to have anything to do with the army anymore. First you started working in a tobacco company as a salesman, then on to M&Ms, thanks to your sister's husband. This job didn't really suit you, so you opened a shop selling spirits with Uncle George, but this wasn't right either.

I have three sisters and a brother. Apparently, my older sister Pascale and I have the same father (I am the second child), but according to our aunt, Pascale has a different father. We never knew who to believe, and only a DNA test could give us an answer. My sister Alexandra is the third child. Her father is unknown to us. Only Alban and Stephanie, the last two, have met their father, but one day he went for cigarettes and never came back. We all look very different, except the two youngest who are very similar. We have always lived more or less separately.

In 1965, I arrived at my foster parents place at around three months old and stayed until I was six. Pascale came too. They had a small house in the suburbs of Nancy. In the corner of the living room there was a wall covered floor to ceiling with key rings and I often sat in front of it, contemplating them. They were all shapes and sizes, some looked like toys, others had magical qualities like changing pictures depending on the angle you looked at it from. It was a true child's paradise. Upstairs was the bedroom where my sister and I slept alongside a beautiful doll as big as a two-year-old, and my brown bear. There we spent a few happy years, as a normal family, with Jeanette and Marcel. They considered us as their children and we wanted for nothing, including love. Maybe because they had no daughters, we were special to them. They took part fully in our lives. At school fetes they photographed us and filmed us as they would with their own children, to keep memories of those moments. They took us everywhere with them, including on camping holidays to the south of France.

They had two teenage boys as well as a younger boy who was placed with them because he was mistreated by his parents. He was a little older than my sister and we were as close as if we had been siblings. In the streets, everyone knew everyone and the kids in the area would meet outside our house at the end of the cul de sac. My sister used to terrorize the other kids by biting their ankles when they got in her way. I'm sure they still remember her...

In 1968, Alexandra came to live with us and our foster parents for a while. My grandparents and aunt only found out about her existence when she was nearly a year old. They did not take the news well and Alexandra sadly suffered the consequences. My aunt never accepted her and always made that very clear. Not only did she have to build her identity without a father, but she also one day found out that her existence was only declared about a year after her birth. This too remains a mystery.

I have very few memories of my mother in that house. I know that she visited us for birthdays and such likes but was often away on tour as a singer. I have no memories of tenderness from her, or any photos or me on her knee or in her arms. But for us life with Jeannette and Marcel was blissful.

In 1971, when I was turned seven, my mother came and tore us from that family for good. We couldn't understand. Pascale cried, she wanted to jump out of the taxi, I didn't want to leave with a stranger. We were ripped from that life without having a choice and we found out later that my mother owed them a lot of money, which is probably why we never went back.

We saw them again many years later. Daniel, Pascale's husband, contacted them for us. Every year Marcel went down to set up his caravan at the Espiguette campsite in the South of France then went back to Nancy to fetch Jeannette. They stayed there from June to September, always in the same spot for years. At the time, when we lived with them, they didn't yet have the caravan, just a huge blue tent. When I see the pictures I can feel the heat of the sand that burnt our feet and smell the fries that Pascale and I went to collect from the campsite bar in a plastic bowl bigger than our two heads together. I remember the stolen pleasure of eating one or two fries on the way back, even though they burnt our tongues. We would go to the beach, make sandcastles and bury Marcel's whole body in the sand. Marcel took us swimming in the sea, where we would cling to him like leeches because we couldn't yet swim. Occasionally my grandmother and my aunt would come and join us and it would feel like real holidays just like any normal person.

In 1991, when Marcel drove his caravan South in April, he stopped on the way to see me. He folded me into his arms and we cried. I couldn't have been happier to see him, all those memories burst forward and I felt like a little girl again.

That summer Pascale, myself, and our husbands joined

them once again on their summer camping break. They had been coming to the same campsite for so long that Marcel worked security in the evenings. It was like their second home. We were so happy to be reunited with our family. They had been as torn apart by the separation as we had and it was a joy to be together again. We talked a lot of what we had been through but I couldn't detect any resentment towards our mother, despite her debts.

Later, we returned to the house where we had spent so much of our childhood. It was as I remembered it. We saw their son and spent an evening talking about the past. I could sense Jeannette and Marcel's discomfort however, as their daughter-in-law had converted her family to Jehovah's witnesses, driving a wedge between Jeannette and Marcel and their grandchildren. We saw Lucas, the younger boy who we had played with as kids and were thrilled to spend time with him even though we had lost that complicity that we had as children.

Marcel suggested watching the home videos he had of us when we were little, which was amazing. It broke my heart though to see so much happiness and to think what our mother tore us from to drag us into her miserable life. We craved that happiness, with a real mother and a real father.

AN EVENTFUL YOUTH

In the early 70s, you decided to join the New York Police Department, while Uncle George joined the firefighters. This was also around the time that your mum introduced you to your future wife. Your future was set.

After Nancy we went to live in Avignon. I remember our neighbour, a rich, man from North Africa, very kind and very respectful, who offered to buy my sister for her blond hair and blue eyes. I feared this man because there was a rumour that he kept a huge snake in his house. I never saw any sign of this animal, but the rumour was strong enough for my child's mind to be convinced of its veracity.

Then on to Banon, near Manosque in the South West, where my mother had a restaurant, which she managed with Alban and Stephanie's father Christian. That is until he disappeared. This is also where I first started to sing, perched on a coffee table with a book of Edith Piaf's music.

In 1973, we moved back to Saint-Etienne, where we lived in various different places, including the "Park with the Red Gate", where one of my mother's exes left our squirrels Aglaé and Sidonie to die of cold on the balcony. Then we lived in "Monthieu" with a man who was involved in organised crime. There was even a newspaper article about him. He wasn't very nice to us, and my brother took the brunt of it.
It was also in this area that I nearly accidentally killed my youngest sister Stephanie. She was only tiny at the time and I was walking her in her crib. To get up to our apartment block there was a long steep slope and I twisted my ankle on the way up. I was only young and my first reaction was to let go of her crib, which started rolling down the hill at speed. It came to a halt inches from a police dispatch car. I felt awful. The cops couldn't understand where this child had come from! My mother was yelling out of the window like an opera star and Stephanie was sitting there giggling. At least she enjoyed it.

In 1974, we left for Clermont-Ferrand with another of my mother's boyfriends, a man who we didn't much like but who we had to live with for 17 years. It was a long and exhausting relationship and took its toll on us three eldest girls. One Christmas stood out in Clermont. I was given a beautiful doll with blond hair and blue eyes, she was dressed all in pink and had lots of little clothes to dress her in. The first time I changed her clothes was a bit of a shock though when I found that this girl doll was in fact a boy doll, with a tiny penis and the face of a girl. It made everyone laugh at first but I got used to it and I kept the doll for many years. I also had my first car accident in Clermont-Ferrand. I crossed the road without looking and flew over the bonnet of the car that hit me. Fortunately there were no broken bones, just a few cuts and bruises.

In 1975 we moved again... and so on and so forth. They say that travelling shapes youth but by this time we were sick of always moving.
It wasn't easy for our mother, life definitely gave her lemons but she never could make the lemonade. Neglected by her men after she had carried their children, she struggled to raise us in a world where it is shameful to be a single mother. We lived with her when we were teenagers but before that we floated from foster homes to hostels to care homes never knowing where we might end up. She was a singer in a cabaret. She had a beautiful voice and she was a beautiful woman and was

extremely successful with men. This meant that she had little time for us as small kids. When we were a little more independent she took us back under her wing, the three eldest. My younger brother and sister went to boarding school where we saw them for the weekends.

I think somewhere along the line she slipped off the rails, got lost in a labyrinth of lies she couldn't escape from. We covered for her so many times, becoming accomplices when faced with her mother, her sister and her future ex boyfriends she borrowed money from. I remember going to collect an envelope from a car downstairs full of money her man had lent her to cover the costs of one of her children's fictional funerals. She wouldn't go herself, as she was "too upset at the loss of her child". I remember the boyfriend telling me he was sorry for my loss and having to make up a story on the spot when I understood what she had done.

I remember a debt collector ringer the buzzer pretending to return my mother's dog, saying it had been hit by a car, then barging into the flat to intimidate my absent mother into giving him his money back.

I remember the hairdresser my sister went to regularly who started asking her to pay my mother's unpaid dues. I remember the poor boyfriend who had to hide in the closet when the "real" boyfriend showed up, asking who she was drinking with. We lied and said it was one of us and we helped boyfriend number one escape unseen...

Sometimes she would lose it and disappear, leaving just a note on the kitchen table. We would call my aunt to help and eventually my mother would return, riddled with guilt. She would tell us about all the trips we would go on, travelling abroad to exotic places... She too needed to escape.

For a long time, I was angry at my mother for what she put us through, but now I don't judge her, she did the best she could. The only thing I regret is the lies she told us, her own kids.

Life was a bit of a rollercoaster through all these years and all these cities. I don't have many happy memories from this time and I have a habit of burying memories that make me uncomfortable. I've closed the door on this part of my past, which was overall pretty boring, to try to move on to the future. It was hard to make friends; I lacked the best friend I needed to confide in because we moved around too much. Fortunately I had my sisters and brother, we lived through the same crap and we were close to one another, we looked out for each other as best we could and kept our mouths shut when any of the others got into trouble.

FIRST SEARCH

One night, you get up and start pacing your apartment. You take the telephone and attempt to make a call to a number in France. Nobody picks up but at least you tried. You try to write, but when Aida approaches you hide what you are writing. She can sense that something is not right. She is worried about you. She asks questions but you can't, or won't, answer. You shut yourself down in your depression. She is scared that it will get so bad that you will try to do something stupid. She is afraid not for herself, but for the children. Maybe you think that because you didn't tell her about your relationship with my mother from the start, now it's too late. Aida suffers in this situation because she doesn't know what is wrong, all she wants is to understand. Now she tells me that everything makes sense. She finally understands where that depression came from that gripped you for six long months.

Pascale and I have thought about searching for you for a long time. Until now we had never tried but this time our minds are made up and we pick up a pen. It is July 17th 1987 and we are going to send our first letter to the Consulate of the United States of America in Lyon. We can't hold back our excitement as we write about who we are and why we are asking for their help. Their answer arrives a few weeks later. They recommend getting in touch with the "Department of the Army" in Washington, which we do immediately. The response is negative, the army wants to help but they need more information such as your full name, rank, military number and social security number, as well as your dates of service in the military, and then contact the National Personal Records in Missouri. This is where all the military archives are kept. It's not going to be easy! We decide to write your curriculum vitae but we are missing so much information! We don't have your date of birth, your social security number and have no idea of your dates of service. Thankfully, we do have your military registration number, which gives us hope so we send another letter to this new address. The letter we receive back tells us that you left the army in 1964 and settled in New York city. It tells us that our letter has been forwarded to your last known address in the Bronx but soon this is returned, as you no longer live there. I look through the minitel looking for a Roberto Rivera in New York but there are so many and I have no idea which one might be you without an address.

One day I receive a letter from Mr Lacy MacCrary, a journalist from the Philadelphia Enquirer. He asks me if I want to do an interview over the phone. I had a friend in the village who spoke English and she agreed to translate the questions and answers. The interview lasted around 15 minutes and Lacy tells me that he will try to help. He is very kind, but there are so many of us in this situation that I don't hold much hope after the call is wrapped up. I'm afraid that our search will come to a dead end, now, and for months I keep watch over the mailbox, hoping for good news. Sadly nothing comes of it.

I've run out of ideas. We didn't have an internet connection at home at the time. I don't know who to contact and out of desperation send a letter to a TV show called "Perdus de Vue" (Lost from sight). The show takes tips about missing people to try to reunite them with their families. My sister and I used to watch it as children, dreaming of being the protagonists, reunited with you. They reply a few months later saying they cannot follow up on my request. They give me the names of two websites I can try. I had already tried them.

Life follows its course, my own kids grow into teenagers. You would have been proud of Karine, my eldest, with her long dark hair with auburn streaks, her beautiful green eyes that put everyone under her spell. You would've liked her strong personality. She is passionate about biochemistry and would like to be a researcher in a laboratory. Once I found a tub of cream in her room covered in mould and when I started to get angry at her she told me the mould was cute and she couldn't wait to analyse it under her microscope. I had no idea what to say to that! Maybe one day she will discover a cure for cancer. You would have been proud too of my son Franck, the younger of my two children. He is tall and broad, a force of nature, with neat short cut hair and sparkling green eyes. Even when he was little he was mad about agriculture. He followed his dad and his grandfather all over their farm. Now he is preparing to take over the farm, become a farmer himself. I think he's very brave; it's not easy working the land these days.

I want them to know how much I love them and how proud I am of them. It took time to have my daughter, but after multiple treatments I was thrilled to have them both, two years apart. I am so lucky to have been able to raise them, see them grow up, take care of them, take them to school, pick them up, help them with their homework and just be with them, making the most of that time. Life goes by so quickly and now they are big it's harder to hug them. Sometimes I wish they were small again so that I could tuck them into the crook of my elbow and they could wrap their little arms around my neck.

In 2004, I separated from their father to start a new life.

It was difficult for the kids to share the time between me and their dad, always between two homes, suitcase in hand. It was hard for me too, especially during the weeks when I was alone. I was fighting life and daily chores until one day I couldn't make ends meet. I was a temp worker and only earned a living when I was working so I didn't get much help from the State, despite my unstable job. When my contract ended and I still had my two kids to feed I panicked. I had to leave them with their dad, I only collected them at weekends until I could find a job. I also had to leave my flat because I couldn't afford it. I certainly didn't want any debts... I felt drained. I've never sunk so low and after all the fighting I finally felt defeated. I missed my children. I had never felt so empty, so broken, so useless. It would be so easy to just give up...

Fortunately my best friend at the time offered to let me live with her. She has enough energy for the two of us and gave me courage, helping me to quickly find a part time job. It's not enough to allow me to move back in with the kids but it helps get me back on my feet. I feel eternally grateful to her. I spent a year with her. She is her own boss and suggested that I help her open a chocolate shop in Saint-Etienne. I accepted, as this meant I could go back to renting my own place and the kids could move back in. I felt relief, my situation was improving, I could finally see the end of the tunnel. This is when I met my husband Gregoire. He gets on great with the kids and they respect him. He can say things without violence and encourages dialogue which is something that really works for us. Our new little family is functional again. After a year the chocolate shop closed and my friend couldn't keep me on. I managed to find a new position in the same sector and all that time I'm thinking of you. I keep searching online and can't find you! Why are there so many people named Roberto Rivera? Artists, judges, businessmen, doctors, dentists, hairdressers, salesmen, bandits... Which one is you? Where are you?

PUERTO RICO

Puerto Rico, the island of your youth. This is where you were born. This is where you grew up, in the town of Ponce. I know you will always be connected to this place and returned regularly. You loved this island...

The plane begins its descent. The hostess tells us in English and in Spanish that we will soon be landing at San Juan airport on the island of Puerto Rico. The sky is clear, the sun is shining on the water and we can see the peninsula of the old harbour looking like a model town from way up in the air. I can't wait to be down on the ground, exploring every inch of your homeland.

I met Greg on May 1st, 2008. We had arranged to meet at the park of the Chateau in Andrézieux Bouthéon in the Loire region. He lived in Grenoble and I lived in the

Plaine du Forez, so I had initially suggested the car park of the stadium in Saint-Etienne (this seemed easiest for everyone) but Greg insisted on the Chateau as he said it would be more romantic for our first meeting. When we first saw each other he immediately took me in his arms and we fell in love there and then. As we got to know each other I told him my story and all about my search for you Dad. Greg wanted to know all about it and asked lots of questions. I told him you were a GI in the US Air Force and that you were born in the town of Ponce in Puerto Rico. When we started talking about getting married two years later he told me that for our honeymoon he would take me there, so that I could discover the land of my origins. I told him it was too far and too expensive, but he was adamant. To him this was something I had to do, even though I didn't yet know it. I can't believe how lucky I am to have found a man so attentive to my happiness and so generous. What a wonderful wedding gift he gave me.

We got married on 18th June 2011 in Langeac in the Haute Loire region. It was a lovely day with a few drops of rain on the way into the city hall and lots of sun on the way out. We received so much love from our families and friends on that day and my husband looked so charming in his beige suit and silk shirt. We couldn't have been happier. Four months later, as promised, we packed our bags and set off across the Atlantic for our dream holiday.

In the past, I had already tried to find you, but I didn't know how to go about it or who to turn to. Life, children and work all contributed to the fact that for around ten years I had stopped looking. My mother had left me a photograph of you in your US Air Force uniform and my aunt had given me two cha-cha CDs where by some miracle your military serial number was inscribed. I tried to use this number to get some information from the army about you but to no avail.

When Greg and I started to plan our trip, Greg asked me whether I wanted to spend some time searching for you, Dad, in Puerto Rico. It was obvious to him that I did. We needed at least your date of birth because without this we were stuck and were going to find it very difficult to get hold of any additional information. He suggested that I write a new letter to the army. The Internet had become a thing by now and they might be better equipped to help me. I once again felt hope that I might find you.

So Greg started searching the web to try to find your date of birth. He found a website for the US Army administration where it is possible to make a request for information. We filled it in and crossed our fingers in the hope that we would receive a response before we left for Puerto Rico. As we were searching the web I also came across an article that troubled me. It mentioned a Roberto Luis Rivera, with a picture of him that I struggled to tear my eyes from. This man had died as a result of exposure during the 9/11 attacks. It mentioned that he left behind a wife and three kids. I remember the feeling of sadness that I felt. I didn't believe it was you, and yet...

Sadly the day of our departure came and we had still received no news from the army. The mail box remained empty apart from bills and ads.

We arrived in San Juan mildly disappointed at having heard nothing but ecstatic at the idea of finally being in this amazing country. The outside of the city is very American but the historical centre of the island's capital has preserved its colonial style buildings. Our first hotel, the "Casablanca", is located in the city centre. The streets are lined with traditional buildings in bright colors and tiny souvenir shops where cigars are still rolled by hand and smell of American and Latino cooking. Before we make our way there, we take the time to visit the San Cristobal fort, an imposing marvel of architecture at the tip of the island.

On Sunday, as we head out to discover the island, we stop in a parking lot by the sea to admire the view. Just next to us is a small bar and we decide to get a drink. The atmosphere is strange and we go to the terrace instead to enjoy the view. There are two other men present, drinking beers. Their faces are weathered in the same way that we have seen on many men on the island. Greg asks them if they would be willing to let us photograph them. Their reaction is very negative and they start to laugh. To relax the atmosphere Greg starts to tell them about my origins in Puerto Rico and gradually a kind smile settles on their faces. We continue to chat across our tables before finally they invite us to their table so I can tell them my story in more detail. They tell us they are father and son and that they don't see one another often. Luis, the older man, explains that he too had a brother in the US Army who went to Germany, and spent some time in Europe. We talked this way for over an hour. Before we left, we took pictures of the three of us to keep a trace of this incredible moment. We understood there and then that whether we found you or not, we would have some amazing memories of this place.

The following Monday, we start our investigation at the administration building of the state of San Juan. We drive around for a while on the administrative blocks before we find the building mentioned to us by the car rental lady. In our average English we speak to the person on the welcome desk who sends us on an epic trip around the building, worthy of a marathon.

"Ask at desk X, go to floor Y and ask Mrs Z" "No it's not me you're after, it's Mr W on the first floor".

Administration is the same in every country... Every time Greg tries to explain our request in his best English. We end up at the desk of a kind looking gentleman who seems touched by my story and starts typing stuff on his keyboard. However despite his willingness to help, he tells us we don't have enough information. There are too many people with the same name to be able to draw any conclusions. So it's a lost cause for today.

The next three days we spend discovering the west of the island, the sandy beaches in Luquillo and the tropical forest of El Yunque. Greg took me kayaking for the first time by night to see a bioluminescent bay. There are only four or five in the world, three of which are in Puerto Rico.

Our next step is the city of Ponce. This is where you were born and grew up Dad.

Our arrival in Ponce is very surprising. The infrastructure around the main cities of the island is very American, with four lane highways in every direction and huge outlet stores like in the US. The most surprising thing is the enormous letters like a Hollywood sign announcing the city entrance. For this step in our voyage we have opted for luxury. We have reserved a room at the Hilton and everything is big and impressive: the pool, the casino, the terrace, even our room with its 2m wide king sized bed.

Once we are settled in, we head out to explore the city. As we approach the centre, the houses get more and more run down and then suddenly we reach the historical centre and the houses are all colorful and in a completely colonial style from the XIXth century. There are lots of people in the square. Children are playing and men and women sit and gossip on the benches enjoying this beautiful sunny day. Latino music is escaping from a restaurant and brightens the whole square with its sound.

Did you feel these strong emotions too? Did you feel the same thing as me when you stood in this square? Were you sensitive to the gentle Latin-American atmosphere with a Caribbean flavour? Even though at that moment I don't know if I am walking in your footsteps, I don't know how long you spent in this city, I don't even know if you liked it but I feel close to you. We explore the cathedral where I later learnt you had been baptised and that you loved. I don't know if it was you that attracted us there but every time we returned to this square we ended up by the cathedral, next to the fire station with its black and red walls that looks like a museum and welcomes tourists.

We spend a while wandering around the square and then Greg bravely decides to go and talk to some guys grouped around a Harley. He tells me the guy on the bike, with the tattoos, huge biceps and a beard, is probably ex-military. He walks over to them, my Dad's picture in hand and asks them if by any chance any of them know the guy in the photo. They recognise him immediately as an army man and the guy on the Harley turns to his skinny friend:

— Hey you were in the army, do you know this guy
— Let's see? No I don't recognise him, where was he based?

Greg tells them about your time in the US army and your time in France. "Come with me, the guy who runs the tourist office was military too."

We start to tell our story once again. Every time there is a lot of emotion on all sides. We felt so much empathy from everyone we spoke to, and every time we saw them disappointed not to be able to help us solve our puzzle.

The man at the tourism office explains that in Ponce there is an ex-military association for the US Army. They meet every Monday in a building outside the city. He gives us a map and marks the place with a cross. Tells us to go ask on his behalf. He also tells us that we can try the local archives. He says "Go see Gladys, she'll be happy to help."

Even though the results don't quite meet my expectations, we are once again surprised at how welcoming the people of this island truly are, and it won't be the last time. But as this trip is also our honeymoon, we go back to the hotel to relax a little, enjoy the pool and have a cocktail. In the evening we head to the casino. The hotel offers $40 of free chips to encourage guests to go and with that we win just over $100 when Greg plays my birthday, the number 26. We have this strange feeling that you are watching over us Dad.

The following morning is dedicated to meeting Gladys at the local archives. Sadly, like in San Juan, the amount of information we have is insufficient and Gladys has to give up the search despite wanting to carry on. She tells us of her experience in Europe in the 60s when she came to take part in the Olympics in Rome. She remembers her stop over in Paris and how this city made her dream. She talked of the lights, the monuments, watching West Side Story in a cinema on the Champs-Elysees. This movie also means something to me. It had informed my grandparents in Saint-Etienne about the life of Puerto Ricans in New York and they were so afraid that if my mother left with my Dad she would be subjected to the same racism and misunderstanding. They were so scared that something would happen to their grandchildren. New York seemed so far away at the time.

New York... I know this city is part of your history. You bought my mother's engagement ring there for a wedding that would never take place. So many memories come bubbling up during that conversation with Gladys, all these questions that remain unanswered. Who were you? What did you become? What happened after France?

In the afternoon we meet with the chief of the ex-GI association in Puerto-Rico. The offices are in a military building, which makes us feel like we're on the set of *Top Gun*. We roam the corridors and eventually find the place where the old GIs meet. There is one of the guys we met in the square in Ponce, who welcomes us and tells our story to his colleagues. They feel touched. Many of them lived through similar experiences, falling in love while on missions abroad. This must bring back fond memories even if they can't talk about it... One of them says: "The boss will meet you".

The boss is also called Luis, it must be a common name on the island. He has a tiny beard and not a hair on his head. We tell him our story and give him your military number. He tells us he was on a base in Asia and wonders whether maybe he too has a son or daughter out there... He says he knows a lot of people in the army and will try to find out what he can for us. I have a strong memory of these moments, all these military men staring at us, wondering what we are doing there and then the look of compassion in their eyes when they hear our story. They are friendly and kind and shake our hands energetically and with great respect. They go above and beyond to be helpful and offer us their seats, coffees... They all try to speak at once and we can tell they all want to share their story. When we leave they wish us luck. This meeting moves me because although these men are a little older than you, you could have been a part of this group.

Afterwards, we go back to our favourite HQ in Ponce: Burger King, just opposite the cathedral. I love their "Double Wopper" and American coffee. Greg, not so much. Most importantly, there is wifi which allows us to search the web for more information and to share our photos of this beautiful place with our family and friends back home. I'm drinking my coffee when I suggest to Greg that we find out whether there is a local newspaper. "What for?", he asks. It has occurred to me that we could post an ad in the paper, with the picture I have of you, and maybe someone will recognise you.

Greg thinks it's worth a try so we ask the waiter which is the most read newspaper around here.
The paper is called "La Perla Del Sur" (The Pearl of the South). Once we have found the address of the building we head over there in our Toyota Yaris. When we get there, it's slap in the middle of an industrial area. We go into the offices where we are met by one of the journalists. He becomes one of the many people touched by our story and tells us that just a few years ago a young German man had come there with a similar request. He explains that this man had been lucky as his father had become an important political figure on the island and he had been able to find him easily. He even ended up settling here and opening a place serving German specialties. He gives us the address and we vow to go and eat there. Once he has heard our story, he writes the article in Spanish and translates it into English for us to approve. It's perfect. He scans the photograph and tells us the ad will appear on Saturday in the next edition of the paper. We will have to spend more time waiting and hoping that someone knows your face and tries to get in touch. It's a needle in a haystack. Even if you came back to Puerto Rico often, what are the chances of someone remembering you? Following that ad we received only one response from somebody willing to help us, but it wasn't very fruitful and the exchanges didn't last long.
The next few days of our trip we spent visiting more of the island, including the magnificent Cabo Roio, where we stayed in an amazing hotel called "Bahia Salinas

Beach Resort". The hotel had a beautiful pool spilling into the sea and we focus on calm and relaxation after all this emotion.

We also spend some time in the North-West of the island, a surf spot where the Atlantic Ocean meets the Caribbean Sea. It's incredible watching the surfers fly over the waves. On our way back to San Juan, we make a detour through the forest to check out the German place. We had a great time there but didn't get any additional information to help us find you. We spend another two days in the capital soaking up the Latino atmosphere and then too soon it is time to go home. Your island is so beautiful! I am sad to leave but feel so thankful that I had the opportunity to be here.

BACK HOME, THE START OF A NEW ADVENTURE

When we get home, the first thing Greg does is fetch the mail. During our trip, he had received an email from the US Army saying they hadn't yet received our request for information in the mail and if they didn't receive it within a few days our request would be void. When he told me this I thought that the world was against me and I would never find you, but in the mailbox there is a letter from the US Army. This is something I wasn't expecting, I am excited and terrified all at once. I turn the envelope over and over in my hands but I can't bring myself to open it. I hand it over to Greg, who tears open the seal. Inside there is a mili-

tary CV. I watch him read and his eyes darken. After a short while he looks up, sadly, and tells me that you have already passed away. I am silent for a few minutes. I can't think. I tell him I suspected as much, that the chances of finding you alive were 50/50, that this is life... But inside I'm in turmoil, nothing makes sense in my mind, thoughts run over one another and everything's a blur. I can feel my kids watching me. I have to stay strong, for them. I keep myself busy preparing dinner and we sit down to eat and talk about trivialities, the conversation animated by the kids. We clear the dishes, tidy up, the kids go off to their dad's and I fall apart. I knew this could happen, but suddenly I know that I will never meet you. I can never tell you how much I miss you, that I have thought about you every day, that you kept me going. I will never get to be held in your arms like a little girl. I had imagined meeting you so often, I could see the moment in my mind like a movie, I knew exactly what I would say to you. It feels like a punch in the gut. All my hopes and illusions are gone, just like that. I was so close, life is playing another trick on me. I feel frustrated, angry, totally disappointed. I feel punished, angry that death took you away before I had the chance to know you even a tiny bit. I hadn't cried for a long time but now the tears come streaming down my face and I can't stop. Greg holds me in his arms and I wonder how you can mourn someone you never knew? How can I live with this?
When the tears dry up and my head is still swimming,

Greg suggests that we continue our research. After all, now we at least know your birthday and that will make things much easier. A few minutes later he tells me he has found an article online talking about your death and I am surprised to see the same article I had come across before we left for Puerto Rico. That feeling I had when I read that article, the feeling that I knew you, that I couldn't tear my eyes away from the picture of you in your uniform, from those dark eyes and hair, just like mine. I had stared long and hard at that photograph looking for a resemblance, without even knowing it was you. It's a shock but I am relieved to finally know that this is you. I ask Greg to translate the article for me. I don't want to miss a thing.

Death Notice found on the Internet

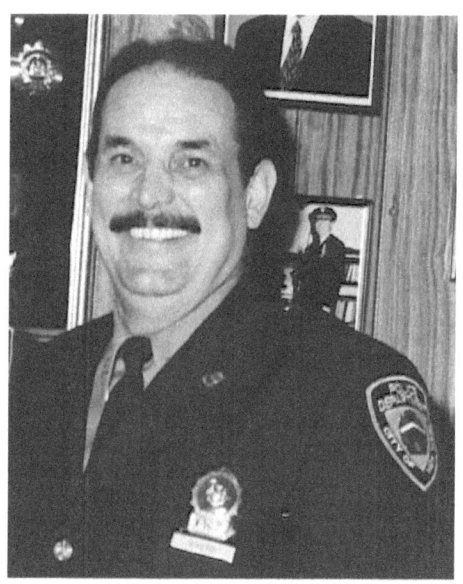

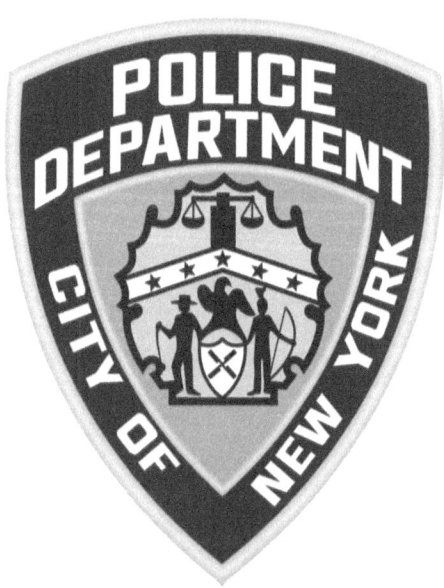

at Puerto Rico's Return

Detective – Roberto L. Rivera
New York City Police Department, New York
End of Watch: Saturday, January 27, 2007

On January 27, 2007, at age 63, Detective 1st Grade "Bobby" Rivera succumbed to illness contracted following the rescue and recovery effort in the aftermath of the 2001 attacks at the World Trade Center.

Born in Ponce, Puerto Rico and resident of the Upper West Side in Manhattan, he was a graduate of Aviation High School and served four years as jet engine mechanic with the U.S. Air Force.

Bobby served thirty years with NYPD including assignments to the 44 Precinct, O.C.C.B., Bronx C.C.I.U. and the Joint Terrorist Task Force where he served twenty years until his retirement in December of 2002. His extensive experience with J.T.T.F. included the investigation of the World Trade Center bombings in 1993 and 2001. Several overseas deployments included investigation of the U.S. Embassy bombings in Kenya and Tanzania and the bombing of the U.S.S. Cole in Yemen. He was also twice deployed to Guantanamo Bay, Cuba for interrogations of terrorist suspects brought back from Afghanistan.

Bobby is survived by his wife Aida and children Marcus, Roberto Jr., and Doraida.

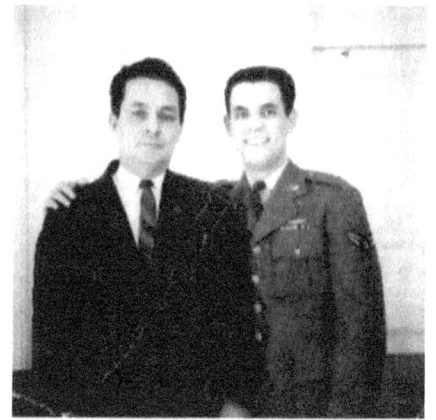

Manuel Rivera, my grandpa, and Daddy

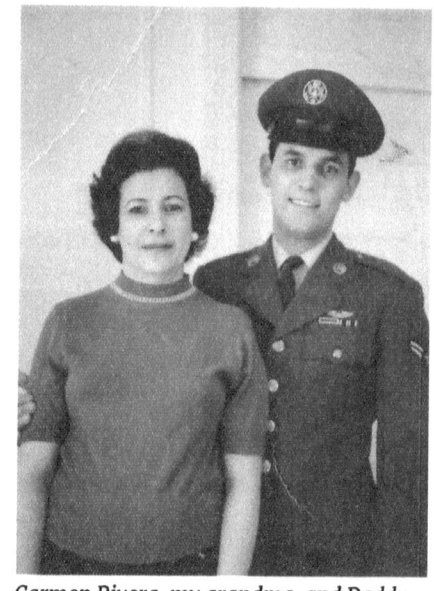

Carmen Rivera, my grandma, and Daddy

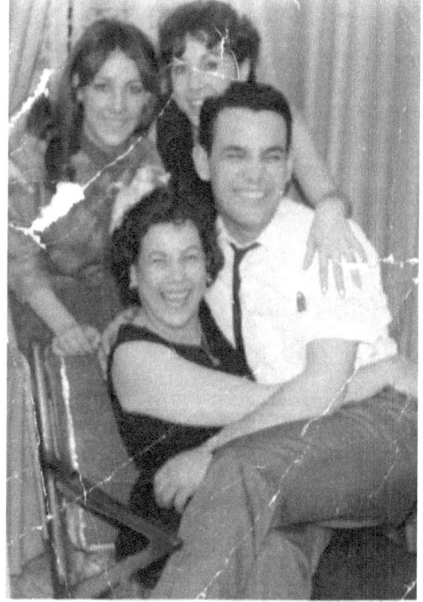

Martha and Margie my Aunts Carmen my Grandma and Dad

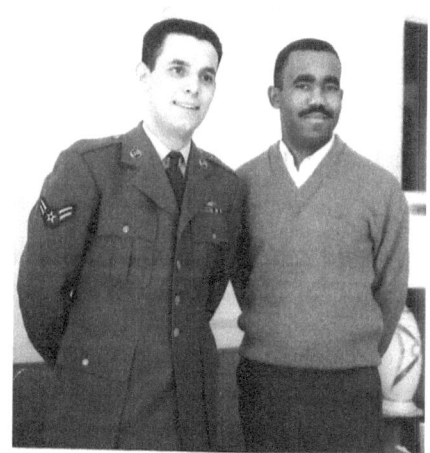

Daddy and Uncle Georges

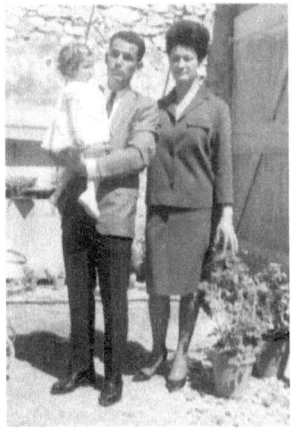
My sister Pascale, my Dad and my mother Michèle Nicolas

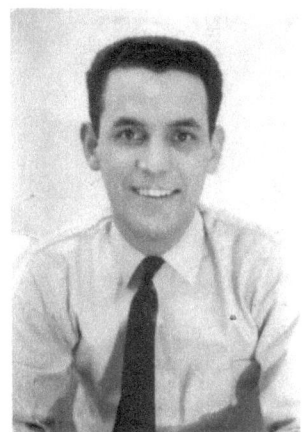
Daddy

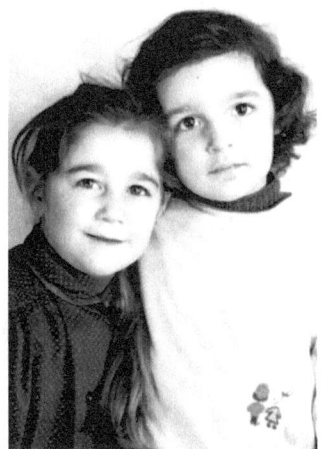
My sister Pascale and me

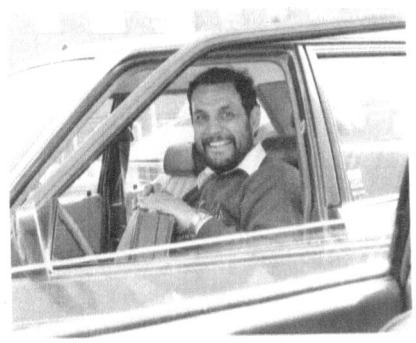
Daddy

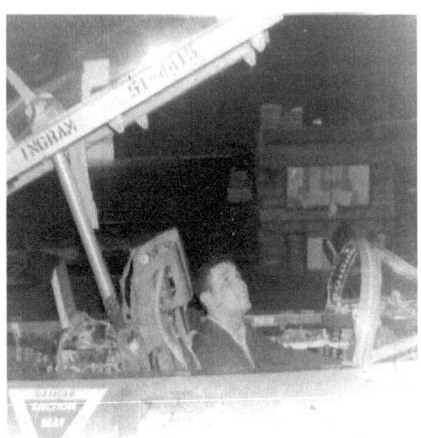

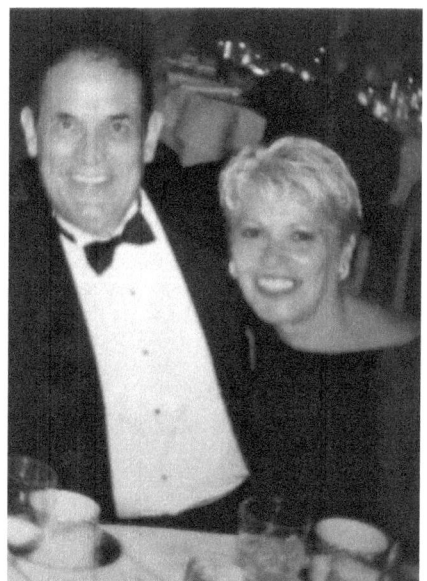

Daddy and Aida

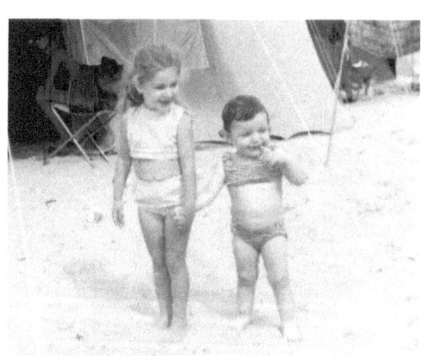

My sister Pascale and me

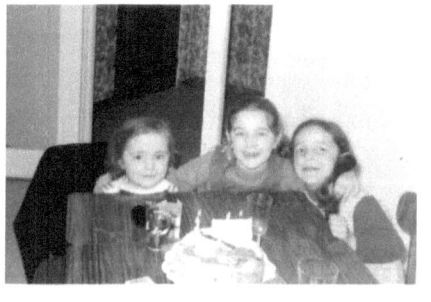

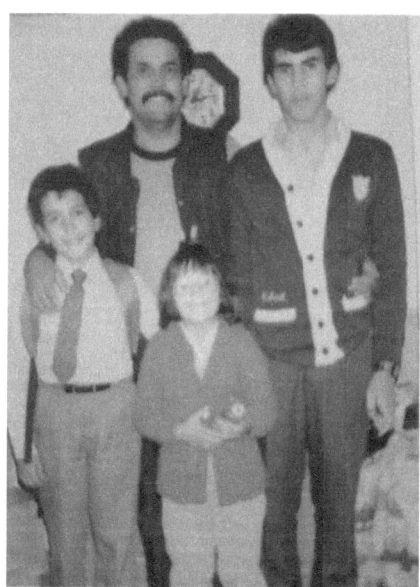

Daddy, my brother Marcus, Robert, Aida and my sister Dori

Daddy, Marcus on the left, Robert Jr on the right, and Dori

My sisters Alexandra, Pascale and me

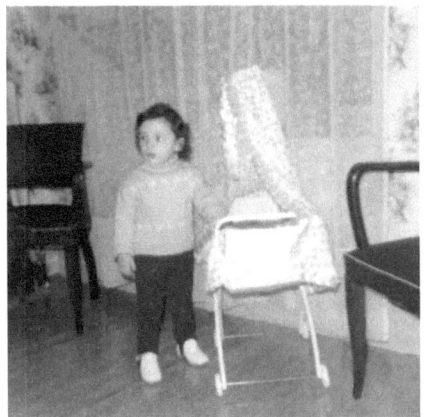

Me

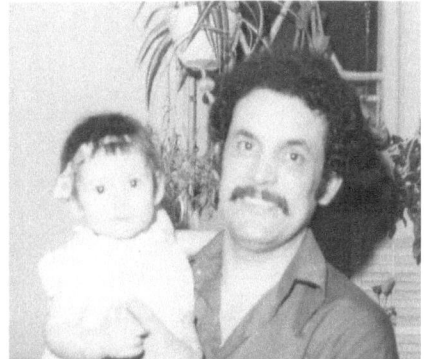

Dori and Daddy

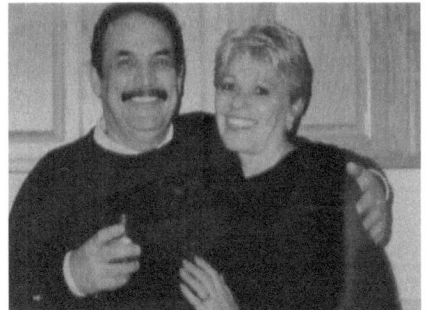

Daddy and Aida

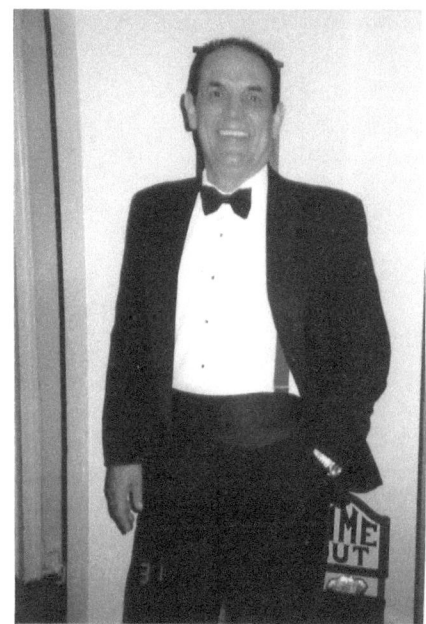

Daddy

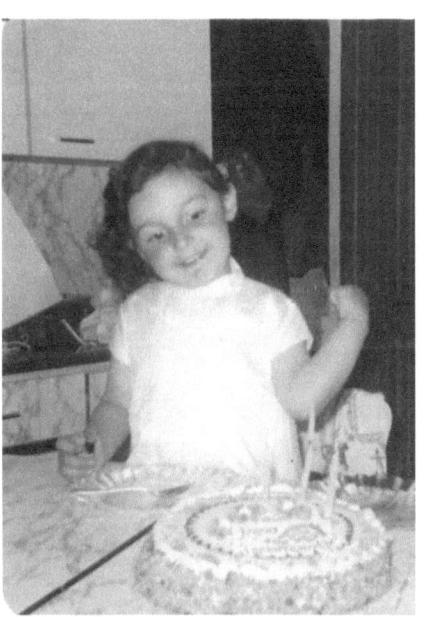

Me

IN SEARCH OF YOUR LIFE

On May 28th 1976, it's dark on 835 Walton Avenue in the Bronx. You have been in the New York police force for just over three years. You and your colleague have just received radio instructions about an emergency at this address. Lawrence Hawkins, a 5-year-old boy, went missing three hours ago. His big sister sent him to take the trash down to the basement. You are now searching the dingy vacant rooms with a flashlight when you come across his body, bathed in a pool of blood. Lawrence was stabbed sixteen times. This story will mark your career, and your life, forever. This is your first murder case. Kenny Ryan, 20, is arrested thirty hours later and confesses to the crime "on an impulse" under the influence of drugs and alcohol. This is your first big case, but not your last. This is how you became an officer in the New York Police.

I am told this story much later. But though article online, we discovered that you were a New York Police Officer and that you died of cancer caused by exposure to the toxic gases and ashes you breathed following 9/11. You died as a hero for your country, recognised only years after the events as a victim of this horrific attack. We discovered that you are survived by a wife and three kids. I discover that I have a family. Minutes ago I lost a father and now I have two brothers and a sister living in New York. A wave of emotion passes over me and I don't know what to feel. I am torn between the immense pain of losing you and the joy of finding people who know you, who can tell me about you. I am scared. How will they react if I try to contact them? Will they want to meet me? Will they accept me? Do they even know I exist?

When I searched for you before I came across so many people with the name Roberto Rivera. I had come across articles about you without knowing it was you because the dates my mother had given me didn't match up. I also read about many other Robertos who had lives far less glorious than your own and I cannot help but feel proud. I would have loved you no matter the life you had led but I feel so honoured to know that you had such a heroic and respectable life. I want to tell everybody about you, about your accomplishments and your role in your community. I could finally talk about you without guessing, I wasn't about to hold back!

First, even though I am terrified, I have to search for your family. I need to find my brothers and my sister, but how?

We spend entire evenings on the internet, looking for information about your life and theirs, we don't know where to start! The web has this advantage and problem, all the information is there, but there is so much of it I don't know how to sort the true from the false, the relevant from the irrelevant. Rivera is such a common name! So we search through the haystack for that one needle. We try to find the right thread that will lead us to you, using the information we have. We consult Look Up and any other website that could give us details.

The first thing we find is a photograph, which after verification seems to be linked to you. It is a picture of Dori and Robert (two of your kids), in spring or summer. It's sunny and they are lightly dressed. She is a beautiful young woman with dark hair and dark eyes and she is leaning down over Robert, in a wheelchair. He too has dark eyes and the same hair but I can't tear my eyes away from the wheelchair. I wonder what happened to him? Is it a permanent disability? Was he born with it? We thought that he too was in the police force so we are surprised and full of questions.

All this information has arrived at once and it has been difficult finding out that you are no longer with us, but I still have your family, and that is precious. I don't know how to contact them, how to approach the subject, tell them about me without hurting their feelings in any way. Will they hate me? Would they reject me? Or just ignore me? After all, I have some of their blood but there was only you, Dad, to link us together. They have no reason to accept me. Every step forward we have taken has brought us to a new obstacle, like a game where a riddle must be answered before the player can move forward. Will we find the right key? My heart is heavy but my hopes are high, and so we start the search for your family.

After contacting all of the police forces in New York, Greg comes across the NYPD Detectives Endowment Association and makes an attempt to contact them. Sam Katz, the president of the association, replies on November 17th 2011, a few days after our request, saying that he is not at liberty to give us your address, but that he can forward our request on to the family.

On November 21st 2011, we receive the first email from Lupe, the wife of Robert Jr, my brother, your son. I am moved by this first interaction, and I want to make sure that we proceed with caution, without rushing anything. Very soon, Lupe asks whether I am Roberto's daughter. The adventure is beginning and from then on we maintain regular correspondence with them. We would like to know everything about them, who they are, and I can't wait to hear from Dori, Marcus and Aida. We understand though that it isn't going to be that easy. Marcus, naturally cautious, is hesitant. He is afraid it may be a scam, so he asks a friend, Stephen Ebbesen, to contact us first:

> Miss Nicolas,
> My name is Stephen Ebbesen, and I represent the Rivera family that you are trying to contact, and have not yet reached. Before they agree to make contact, the Family has asked me to verify your intent. Please answer the following questions;
> Are you attempting to make contact with certain members of the Rivera family?
> If so, why are you interested in contacting the family?
> You may respond to this email. Thank you.
> Stephen Ebbesen
> Ebbesen Intelligence

In his following email he explains that Roberto Luis Rivera was a decorated and respected individual in the community of New York, he has worked on numerous important cases, including terrorist attempts and attacks on New York. He explains that the family are very proud of this and as they know nothing about me they are reluctant to enter into contact. He sends us a list of questions to answer, asking for proof of my relation to the Rivera family. The wait for an answer seems interminable but on December 19th 2011, I find that Christmas has come early when he forwards me Marcus' email address. I am thrilled! What a victory! I can finally meet my family!

Marcus writes back soon afterwards, telling me about his, Dori's and Robert's life with you, Dad. He tells me how much they loved you, what a great father you were and how you were their role model. You were a fun, caring person, and he tells me how growing up was full of love and laughter. He also tells me about your professional life, as a street officer in the NYPD and then part of the FBI's Joint Terrorism Task Force. You were admired, respected and considered a hero by your peers. Marcus tells me how proud he was to work alongside you and his brother at Ground Zero after the 9/11 attacks. He tells me about the illness that killed you caused by the toxic gases. I read and re-read that email a thousand times. It made me so happy, and at the same time was so painful...

Later I received the email from Dori. My eyes fill with tears as she describes what a wonderful father you were to them. She says that knowing the kind of man you were, she was certain that you thought about me every day of your life. She always knew that there was something missing and now she knows that that something was me. She writes: "Oh Fabienne, my sister, YAY!!!!! Finally, I Have One" and I am overwhelmed. I am so happy to know that they want to know more about my family and me and that we are now a part of theirs!

NEW YORK: THE DISCOVERY

You were born on February 27th, 1943, in the small town of Ponce on the island of Puerto Rico. It is the town of your childhood, where you were born and baptised. At this time, life is hard on the island. You are the first child in your family followed a few years later by your sisters Margie and Martha. Your father Manuel is frivolous and rarely at home, which is why your mother Carmen decided to move to New York with you and the girls to look for the American Dream, or at least find an easier life. Uncle George goes with you on this trip. He is a child barely older than you, your mother's brother who she took under her wing. He will grow up to be like a big brother to you.

I know very little about your life in New York until you decided to join the US Army in 1961. I have a trace of this thanks to the journal that you started to write a few years before your death.

I don't remember exactly when my mother and her sister started telling us about you, but the words "military", 'US Air Force", "Puerto Rico" and "New York" resonated in my mind for a long time. You were my hero, the person that I dreamed about as a little girl. In bed at night I would close my eyes and see you as you were in the only photo I had of you, in your uniform. I would imagine you smiling at me, holding me in your arms, resting my head on your safe, strong shoulder. You would rock me gently and I imagined falling asleep listening to your heartbeat. I didn't talk about you much because the kids at school made fun of me and called me a liar. I didn't have a best friend because we moved around too much to make one so my only escape was to dream. At school the teachers often said of me that I had my head in the clouds, I know I was up there with you. They couldn't understand. You were such a hero, tall, strong, handsome, and destined to save the world. I thought that at any moment you would come and get me, no problem. I looked for you in faces on the street, people waiting at the school gates, I listened to the voices in the house when I got home, just in case this time one of them was yours. But you couldn't be with me and at the same time travel the world. It was hard as a child believing these things only for them never to happen. I would have loved to run and play with you, for you to teach me how to swim or ride a bike, or just be near you. I treasured and protected that photograph I had of you in your uniform, standing by your father, just like the white gold engagement ring with the missing diamond. It was kept in a blue velvet box with a white interior with the gold lettering of the jewellery store in New York where you bought it, along with the wedding ring that my sister has. You were even meant to get married. Why didn't it happen? Those were my most valued possessions, along with the two cha-cha CDs I had. They were the only things that linked me to you. When I touched them I felt like I was nearer to you, I kept dreaming about what my life would have been like with you in the United States of America…

And now here we are, taking off from Amsterdam on our way to New York. Marcus will pick us up, myself, Greg, Pascale and Karine, from the airport. My head is swimming, I'm impatient to arrive. I think of all the discoveries we've made in the last few months after being stuck for nearly twenty years. I discover New York from above and my heart stops at the beauty of it. I haven't even touched down and I already love this city. It's a bit like going home. It's the same sensation as I had in San Juan in Puerto Rico. I feel at home.

In the hall of the airport, Marcus is waiting for us.

I see him to our left as soon as we arrive and my heart speeds up. My stomach feels tight, I can feel myself shaking and I try very hard not to cry. He smiles and I look at him, unable to peel my eyes away from his big dark eyes. He looks so much like you. We greet one another and it's a great moment of emotion for everyone. We hug timidly, not really knowing what to say, where to start. It's magical being here, it's so good to see him and it feels like I'm seeing you. We stand in the arrival hall exchanging pleasantries for a few minutes and then Marcus drives us back to your house.

As we have arrived in the evening, he drives us through Time Square and Broadway to give us a glimpse of the heart of New York. It's beautiful, everything is lit up and sparkling. There are people everywhere and we don't know where to look. It's incredible, full of life and it makes me feel dizzy. Eventually we arrive at Clarmont Avenue, a wide street lined with trees and apartment buildings the way we pictured. We are in Manhattan, right next to the University of Columbia and close to Harlem and 124th Avenue. We go into the first hall, where the buzzer looks like it's from the 50s, then into the main hall and over to the elevator. Marcus tells us that Carmen, our grandmother, lived in the apartment on the left at the end of the corridor. We go up in a modern looking elevator and when the doors open I am greeted with a cry of "Aaaaaaaabiiiiie!!" It's my little sister Dori, who has been waiting for us impatiently. We fall into each other's arms, I am so happy! Dori could be in the movies she is so beautiful, a real star; I love her and her three boys immediately. Carl, the oldest is already a tall boy, passionate about cinema. Raymond, the second, is shy and loves video games, and finally Robert, a little ball of energy who doesn't really want to see us as we can tell by his cries of "Go way!". He is adorable and I badly want to shower him with love but he won't let us near him, he's a little rebel.

It feels strange to be in your apartment and discover your home. When we enter there is a long corridor with an old wooden floor that creaks under our weight. There is a big bedroom on the left with two large wardrobes and windows opening onto the courtyard below. Then there is the bathroom followed by a small kitchen and a bar. The living room has black and white photographs of New York adorning its walls, then at the back, on the right is your bedroom. This is where we will be sleeping, in your bed. It's a beautiful room with a big bed covered in cushions. It's very high and we giggle as Greg and I, who are not very tall, try to clamber into it. On the dresser are many photos of your children, Robert, Marcus and Dori, and your great grandchildren as well as your wife, Aida. She is not here because she is away on holiday in the Dominican Republic, but she is loaning us her home without even knowing us. Her generosity blows me away. We listen to the noises of the street, the alarms of the ambulances and cop cars, which seem familiar from so many movies set in the city. We sit on the sofa, Pascale and Karine on my left, Marcus on my right and Dori in front of me, next to Greg. On the floor they have laid out lots of boxes of all shapes and sizes. They are adorable, but it's the contents that we are here for. They are stuffed full of photographs that you have taken here and there of the family, and of places you have been. Dori and Marcus talk about you, they show us the pictures and we are hanging off every word. We want to know everything about you, to enter your world a little bit and try to get to know you. We are exhausted from the trip but so happy to be here, hearing you talked about as a father, a husband, a professional... A bit later I fall asleep in your bed like a little girl and my dreams are full of you.

The next day, Karine is sick. We're off to a good start. We hope she will be better soon as this trip is also her 18th birthday present. It would be a shame for her not to make the most of it! She decides to stay at the apartment and fortunately Dori brings her the medication she needs to get better quickly. Pascale, Greg and I head off on foot to explore Manhattan. We walk a lot during these few days in New York, sometimes just the four of us and sometimes with Dori and her boys. We create good memories there. Dori takes us to strategic places so we can take the same photographs that you took with your family. Whenever Marcus has a moment free he comes and spends some time with us, he shows us his work place, takes us to his office which is very light and airy with a great view. From here you could probably see the Twin Towers. On the right when entering there is a small sofa where Marcus rests when he doesn't have time to go home. On the left of his desk is a cabinet where he displays photos, souvenirs and badges from different departments he has worked for. It feels like we're in an American cop movie, I'm impressed.

He introduces us to his colleagues and his boss, who chats with us for a while. They are all very friendly and we feel welcome. We visit their briefing room where the walls are adorned with pictures of arrested criminals. Then we visit the lab, which is full of James Bond style gadgets, it's odd for us, we're not used to this! We are like kids in a candy store! We go into the interrogation room, a bright white room with the board on the wall where they take mugshots. Karine stands in front of it holding the board with the date on it and has her picture taken. It's a lot of fun for those of us who are innocent. I feel so proud to be walking beside Marcus in the street, even if it's only to go grab dinner from Five Guys or go to his favourite cookie store.

A few days after we arrive, Marcus comes to collect us to take us to meet his family. On the way there, he takes a detour and I can guess where we're going. My heart beats in a frenzy as I realise he is taking us to your final resting place, the place that will hopefully help me to get closure. At the entrance to the huge George Washington Memorial Park Cemetery is an imposing statue of the first American president kneeling in prayer. It is beautiful and peaceful and the cemetery is well kept with a bright green lawn. The weather is sunny and pleasant. The park houses many statues, paintings and bronze sculptures honouring General Washington and his monument, the pillar of courageous men. It's a beautiful afternoon to come and see you. When the car comes to a halt, we get out and follow Marcus across the grass. I'm struggling to walk on this lawn as I'm worried about stepping on people's graves. When we finally get to yours I feel the tears come to my eyes. I stay standing but really I want to sit by you and talk to you for hours. I have so much to tell you, I want to touch your name engraved in the marble but I don't, for fear of embarrassment maybe, or of making my brother, husband, sister and daughter uncomfortable. I stand there, my head down, shoulders hunched and my hair hiding my face, I cry in silence. I feel a hand gently rest on my shoulder and look up to see Marcus by my side. Thank you, my brother, for this support. I look around and see that you are sheltered by an old tree that protects you from the sun and the cold. Rest in peace Dad, you have earned it.

My thoughts drift as I stare at your gravestone and I wonder what things would have been like if you had still been here when I found you. I think about what it would have been like if you had been among us. You would have probably picked us up from the airport, I would have watched you closely, trying to detect joy and even love in your eyes. I would have felt like a child and been intimidated by your presence. I would have been worried that you felt obligated to meet me, but I would have hoped with all my heart that you would have welcomed me with open arms, hugged me and let me rest my head on your shoulder. I would have cried with tears of built up suffering but also relief at finally being with you. I would have thanked God for giving me the opportunity to finally meet you. It would have been amazing to spend these few days with you in New York, so that you could tell us about your life, your family, your work, and answer some of the questions I have been asking myself all my life… Why did you never come for me? I felt some residual anger from my childhood, which thankfully dissipated quickly when I met my new family. We could have got to know one another, laughed and cried together and we would have built our own memories together. My love for you would be as unconditional as ever. You would have shown us the city and the places you liked to go. Your friends would have told us about you and I would never have got bored of hearing about you. We would have talked about music, cinema and your work, you would have shown us your home, your corner of peace "La Casita". I would never have left your side during our time in New York, as if I

could make up for all the years that we lost. I would have made you promise to come to France and I would have visited you often in your country, so close to my heart...
Suddenly Marcus interrupts my reverie and brings me back to reality. It's time to say goodbye.

The evening passes in a joyful atmosphere. Marcus' home is beautiful, typically American, made of wood with a warm, welcoming interior. Melissa, his wife, is stunning, slim and dark haired with fine features and big blue eyes. She receives us with open arms and introduces us to their twins. Their daughter is a shy little girl with long dark hair and big brown eyes who looks like her mother, and their son, with his laughing eyes and cheeky air, is just like his Dad. Melissa has pulled out all the stops and prepared a fantastic dinner which she serves on a beautifully laid table, as if it were a big celebration. It's a challenge for her to receive French people in her home, as she is a big fan of French culture. They tell us that they have been to Paris in the past and have very fond memories of the place. We start the evening with drinks in the small living room which opens onto a large open plan kitchen. Marcus opens a good bottle of red wine and we bask in the pleasure of sharing this moment together.
Before we sit down to eat, my niece rushes to show Pascale, Karine and me her collection of dolls, and my nephew seizes the opportunity to show off his Hot

Wheels collection to Greg. During the meal I try to talk a little more than usual as my spoken English is very poor but I can understand most of the conversation. There are so many things I want to say! Thankfully, Greg is there, he is the only one of us who speaks English well. The conversation remains joyful and they are happy to tell us about their family and their life. They ask us many questions about everything and the evening passes without a pause. Suddenly it's time to go and we realise that we have had our first ever family meal with our American relatives.

The next day we meet Lupe and Robert, my second brother. Robert no longer has any contact with Aida and Dori and the latter two suffer greatly from this. My little brother, who is two feet taller than me, is in a wheelchair following a road traffic accident a few years before. I can't wait to meet him. The first time, we meet on Broadway on an intersection. While we are waiting for them, we notice that a television series is being filmed a couple of blocks away from us. We try in vain to guess which film it is, which occupies us until we see them arriving. Lupe is a tiny woman who radiates energy and beauty. Her huge smile is reflected in her big dark eyes as she pushes my brother towards us. What emotion to finally see them after all this time sending emails! It's cold out so we quickly follow them to the restaurant that Lupe has booked for us. I sit just opposite my little brother so that I can hold his hand, meet his eyes and communicate with him. We decide then to meet again the next day at their place in Queens. I can't wait!

In the evening, Dori gives me a postcard that has been torn in half. I look at her questioningly and she explains that it was a card sent by my mother for your name day, inside it reads: "Your daughters wish you a happy birthday and they are waiting for you." She also hands me a photograph where I recognise my mother. Dori explains that she had seen this stuff at her grandmother's place and asked a lot of questions which remained unanswered. Why did Carmen keep these documents? She knew she had grandchildren in France. And you, Dad, did you ever receive the card and the photo or did she hide them from you? And the biggest question I have asked myself all these years, did you even know I existed? According to my aunt, yes you knew. She says that she sent you a telegram when I was born and that you replied that you were happy. But is this true? It's hard to say and my gut says we will never know for certain. Aida found the card and the photograph when she was clearing out your mother's apartment when she moved into a retirement home. Had you told her that there was someone in your life when you were in France? When she found the card she must not have known what to do, she must have had so many questions and in the moment tore it in half, fearing bringing up ghosts of the past. She must have regretted it though because for some reason she kept it and the photo. She never mentioned it to you. These two documents are tangible proof that you knew my mother, and it is important for your family to know that.

After two weeks spent in your environment, it is sadly time to go back to France. Leaving Clarmont Avenue is hard, but life must follow its course.

SECOND TRIP TO NEW YORK: AIDA AND *LA CASITA*

When you and Aida got married, you spent your honeymoon in the region of Pocono in Pennsylvania. You fell in love and decided to build your second home there with your own hands, to come and rest and enjoy time during the holidays. How many photos I have seen of this place from beginning of construction to the end. How many moments of happiness you must have shared with your family in this incredible place, enjoying the forest, the pool, your friends, your safe haven *La Casita*. I can't wait to discover your little house in the woods.

The second time we make the trip to the US we go with Franck. We want him too to discover his origins and meet his American family. We decide to travel via Montreal because Greg's cousin Emeline lives there. It is a good opportunity to go and visit her and to explore the city. We love it! It's very American but still maintains its French aspects. We are surprised for example to hear the word "Depanneur" used for a small convenience store, or "Nettoyeurs" for a cleaners and the word "ARRET" which replaces the STOP on road signs. It's entertaining when you don't expect it. People are very friendly. Emeline introduces us to "Poutine" (fries with cheese and their super secret sauce), it's delicious and I can see it as a dish that you would eat when you are down, it can only cheer you up! We discovered the Mont Royal area, with its small two or three floor apartment blocks with the metal fire escapes hanging off, just like in New York. We went shopping and while I tried on clothes in the fitting rooms, they tried on ladies clothes in the middle of the shop all the while commenting their outfits. How we laughed!

Two days later we took the road to New York. We thought that this would be a great way to show Franck, who's not a fan of cities, a little bit of the US. Everything we saw was stunning; it's a beautiful part of the country. He also appreciated the young waitress' smile at the diner where we stopped to eat, so we took a picture of them to immortalise the moment. In the evening we needed to find a place to stay. We drove along the road through Albany but not a motel in sight. Suddenly Franck cries out: "I saw one! On the left!". Greg makes a U-turn and we enter a small dirt road where there is indeed an unlit sign that reads "Motel". It feels like we're in a horror movie, I'm terrified. It's raining a little by this time and the parking lot is dark. We go to knock at the door and a voice comes from deep inside: "Yeeaaahhh?". We feel very unsettled... Then the owner appears from nowhere. In the dark we didn't see him coming. He says: "Yeah I have one available", and takes us to see the room. When he opens the doors my stomach turns over, a pungent smell of damp, mould and cold cigarette drifts from the room and it's all I can do to not be sick. The furniture is mismatched and the bathroom looks as though nobody has ever washed in there, and who would want to. We have told him, and he has seen, that there are three of us yet there is just one double bed. From inside we can hear the neighbours fighting about something or other. We turn on our heels and leave, I can just picture Norman Bates dressed as his mother appearing from nowhere with a large knife... What an adventure!

When we finally arrive in New Jersey, a few miles before the George Washington Bridge, we can see the Big Apple from a distance. I turn to Franck and exclaim: "Look! Welcome to New York!". We are all so excited! The bridge we cross has two stories and we take the second so that we can enjoy the view. I am finally going to meet Aida, my Dad's wife, the mother of my brothers and sister! This wonderful woman, who I was so scared of hurting with my existence, the one who told me that I was a victim and could never hate me, and agreed to meet me today.

We arrive at your place and Aida welcomes us with a big smile. She is all done up, make-up, hair, and she exudes happiness. We hug, and the tears escape my eyes without me wanting them to. Aida tells me to smile, it is a day for joy, but I can't help myself, the emotion is so strong.

Aida lends us your room, she will sleep in the living room and Franck will have the guest room. When we protest, she tells us that she is the commander and the debate is over. She has such character! Then she gives me the most incredible gift, your ring, the one you received when you graduated from military school and can be seen in almost all the photographs of you. She also gives me the wings that were attached to your uniform, along with a tag carrying your police registration number. I wear it now around my neck and will never take it off.

We have dinner and spend the evening talking about you. The next day, we meet up with Marcus, Melissa and the kids to visit the Intrepid, a magnificent navy carrier bearing an impressive collection of military planes from around the world. We also visit a submarine dating from the end of WWII.

We go back to visit you at the cemetery and I leave a sunflower on your grave to catch the sun and keep you warm. After visiting the stores in New Jersey with Franck, who is now newly clothed from head to toe (thank goodness he came with an empty bag!), we head over to Pocono, to see *La Casita*. We get a bit lost on the way and the satnav lent to us by Aida takes us on a 40 mile detour before telling us we have arrived when we're in the middle of the freeway! We turn back and come off the road where Greg suggested, and he is right, but it's still not easy to find the house! It's getting dark. We pass by the correct road twice and even with Aida calling to try to help us, Greg is so tired he can't understand much over the phone. Dori and Marcus start getting worried and Dori even started to say that she would come out to find us, but fortunately a little while later we find it! Aida meets us in a big parking lot by the pool. We have finally reached *La Casita*. It is a beautiful house in the middle of the forest, like you would expect in an American movie. A big lounge with a fireplace opens onto a small kitchen decorated in bottle green. At the back is your office, with walls covered in pictures of you, your colleagues and the places you have worked. It feels like a sanctuary and I'm overwhelmed by it all. It feels safe, and I feel close to you.

In the lounge there is a glass cabinet containing the flag that was placed on your coffin, medals won and earned, a picture of you smiling and one of your mother, a small pot containing her ashes, everything that showed your worth and carried memories for your family.

Upstairs there are two bedrooms and Aida once again lets us use your room. In the morning she asks me which side I slept on and I'm pleased when she tells me that it was your side. Downstairs there are also two or three big rooms, the place is designed to welcome a big family. In the daylight, the house in the woods is even more impressive. Aida explains that it's like a little community, they have bracelets that give them access to the pool and she lends us some to show that we are guests here. Everything is in communion with nature. You must have been so proud to build this piece of paradise with your own hands.

Marc and Melissa meet us the following day and we go to visit the Bunskill Falls, a place in the middle of the woods where we could meet all manner of creatures, including brown bears! Marc worked there as a teenager and is happy to show us around. It's so nice just walking through the woods with my brother, his wife and the kids. My niece even holds my hand for a while, which makes me feel proud. Dori and the children will be with us later in the day but Marc and Melissa must head home this evening. My heart drops as I know I won't see them again on this trip as we are not going back via New York, but the time they have set aside for us has been precious. I don't know if they realise how much this means to me.

The next day we set off with Dori and her kids to climb a mountain and take the same picture that Marc and Bobby have from when they were younger. It was a challenge but I succeeded in getting to the top. The view from up there is spectacular; the cars in the distance seem so small! We take many photos, which we will treasure for a long time. On our way back down, Dori takes us to the place where you like to have lunch. She explains that when you passed away, the place closed down and only reopened recently. I see it as a sign that I was meant to visit your favourite places. Typical of the 50s, the interior feels like the inside of a bus, very narrow, with an aluminium bar and blue neon lights. We had an amazing burger that was well deserved after the mountain climb through the Pennsylvanian forest!

The day before we are due to leave, Aida prepares a typically Puerto Rican meal, which tastes incredible. Dori tells us she has not cooked like that for years. She also gives me a Puerto Rican cookbook, in which she has written an inscription. It's a beautiful gift. We must try out this style of cooking! But apparently not your cooking because even though you loved to try you were not always the most successful cook and your family did everything to keep you out of the kitchen…!

We have had a wonderful time in your paradise and must now head back to France. We know though that we will be back soon.

THIRD TRIP TO NEW YORK: OUR THEORY CONFIRMED...

Pascale and I didn't have many pictures of you, but the ones we had were like treasure to us. The one that stands out though was taken when the entire Nicolas family was gathered at Vaison la Romaine and you were there too. The picture shows my mother, and you holding Pascale in your arms. It breathes happiness and calm and you look like a normal family. Sadly that happiness didn't last long after your holiday came to an end.

My uncle liked you a lot, even though you didn't speak the same language. You had that common experience of being bred by the army. My uncle Jean had seen war in Indochina, you had been in the US Air Force and I think that patriotic spirit is the same whatever the country you fight for. You understood one another.

On Wednesday, January 7th 2015, it is France's turn to be touched by horror. The Parisian office of the newspaper Charlie Hebdo is savagely attacked by members of ISIS, in the middle of a conference. Twelve people lose their lives in a matter of minutes, killed by lunatics who wish to avenge their prophet who has been insulted by the satire of the paper. In the following days, more people die at the hands of these brutes. A young police woman in the wrong place at the wrong time and four more people in a hostage situation when the manhunt gets out of hand. France is mourning its 17 victims, some that we did not know, others who were known to all, such as the illustrator and journalist Cabu, who has been drawing for as long as I can remember. Sadness, fear, anger and disgust grip the country and the French population joins together to protest this attack on our freedom of expression and explain "Je suis Charlie" (I am Charlie). This phrase is soon to be seen everywhere, as a tribute to the victims, but also to show that we will not be silenced by these criminals.

How does a human do that to other humans? In the

name of what? Of who? What are these people made of to be able to wreak havoc and destroy lives with no consideration for the families and friends affected? Why is so much hatred born for people who are simply different?

Where are understanding, compassion, and love for the human race as a whole? What are we becoming? The only flame of hope I felt on that day was from the text message I received from Marcus, which read simply "I am Charlie".

In two days it will be my 50th birthday. It's Thursday, April 24th at 1pm. I receive a phone call at work from Greg, who says: "When you leave work this evening, leave your house keys with Melanie, clear your desk and get home quick. You have to pack."

I'm so excited, I ask Melanie what is going on, I ask my daughter via text, but I always get the same response: I don't know! The afternoon drags on and I still can't get any information from anyone. When I get home I ask Greg a thousand questions, so he tells me we are going to Ardeche, a few hours South in France. I think what a nice thing he has organised, a little weekend break away just the two of us, but then I see him get out the big suitcase and start packing it full as though we will be away for a long time and I start asking more questions. He tells me we are going to my sister Pascale's so I call her to ask what time we should arrive.

I can hear the excitement in her voice and I have a feeling that the Ardeche we are going to is actually nowhere near France, it's thousands of miles away and is actually called NEW YORK!! What an incredible gift! I am going to see my brother, my sister, and their wonderful mother as well as my nieces and nephews and everyone I love. I can't wait!

Like we did with Franck, we go through Montreal. When we arrive it is 4 degrees Celsius. We haven't really packed for such cold weather but never mind. It's my brother in law Daniel's first time in the USA and the drive from Canada is ideal to get a first taste. We are happy to see Emeline again. She is a positive, sociable woman who loves people and has a great outlook on life, which shows through her words and her actions. We share a peaceful evening over a Poutine and enjoy listening to her gentle Canadian accent. We have rented an apartment from one of her friends for one night on arrival and two nights when we leave. It feels strange moving into this place that still has all her things in it. She must be very trusting to let us, complete strangers, stay here. In France we doubt everything and everyone, we are impatient, aggressive and angry. We use our car horns liberally and don't respect anyone, whether it is the pregnant lady or the old man trying to cross the street. I'm embarrassed when I think about the lack of respect French people have for others when compared with Canadians or Americans. Here when there is traffic everyone bites their tongues and waits patiently. People are polite and greet each other in the street. If I were younger I would move there to live.

Our trip to New York goes by without any hiccups. It's not very warm but the sun is still present. My sister and I discover that the seats in the back of the rental car are heated, which is very pleasant. We quickly switch them off though when we detect a burning smell, even though it's a new car! We watch the scenery and around 1pm we stop at an Irish restaurant for lunch. We get to New York late afternoon and it's warmer than Montreal. It's such a pleasure to be back with Aida, in your home Dad.

Aida is just as smiling as last time. She is well dressed and her make up is perfect. Her words are generous and her attitude is welcoming, she has a great sense of humour. She lives with her little dog, TJ, a Schnauzer who makes himself heard whenever anyone gets too close to the front door. It's reassuring for someone who lives alone. She also has a cat and the birds that her mother left her. It's so good to see her again! The next day, on my birthday, she gives me a pile of papers and tells me it's my birthday gift. It takes me a while to understand that it is a DNA testing kit. I can't thank her enough! In France it would have been impossible. We would have needed a judge to make the request and knowing the system in France I know it would have been a lost cause.

We would have spent all our money on lawyers and wouldn't have been able to travel to New York. We could have waited years for a test without any guarantee of a result. It's a beautiful gift, and my sister and I are impatient to take it to reassure your family, Dad, but also to settle that burning question: are we really your daughters? Our mother lied so much and so often that we had no guarantee, and our aunt had told us that Pascale was not your daughter. We want to know. I know Pascale is scared but the need for an answer is greater than the fear of a negative one. Four of us take the test. Aida, Marcus, Pascale, and me. We hold such great hope.

To celebrate my birthday, we all go out to an Italian restaurant where Marcus baptised his twins. I wasn't in on the surprise so it's with great excitement that we meet them all again. The kids have grown and changed and I am thrilled to be with them all again. The family are pleased to meet Daniel, Pascale's husband and he fits right in. My brother, Melissa and the kids give me a heart-shaped jewellery box with all our names engraved on top around the inscription "We are family". I am very moved by this gesture, and so touched that they have accepted so openly when they could have turned me away without a second thought.

After this very emotional day, we head back to New York where we plan to stay a few days to visit with

Daniel. We walk for miles between Liberty Tower, Wall Street and Brooklyn Bridge, where Marcus meets us to cross it together. It's a splendid bridge with two lanes on either side for vehicles and a raised passage in the middle for pedestrians and cyclists. The view is sublime. On the right is the port with its orange ferry to take passengers to Staten Island and the One World Trade Center, or Freedom Tower, which stands in the stead of the Twin Towers. It's great to see it finished, standing tall, its glass panes reflecting the clouds and the city. It screams pride from the top of the 104th floor and its gigantic antenna on top. 541 metres in total! The Statue of Liberty looks small from here, guardian of Manhattan Island. On the left are Manhattan Bridge and the East River which separates Manhattan Island from the rest of the continent. And in front of us is Brooklyn. From the bridge, Marcus points out his place of work, and the courthouse and tells us that as we speak a man is being judged there for a number of robberies in the city. Marcus suggests that we go and watch the trial for a while, as he knows that depending on what is said in trial, he may have to start new investigations at any moment. He can't stray too far. It's very impressive: the defendant's lawyers on the right in their gowns, and there are many of them, a criminal investigation team in the centre (which my brother is a member of) and on the left, the jury. There are twelve of them standing just in front of the speaking lawyer. To the left of the jury is the defendant with his translator, then the judge. We look around in awe, as we are not used to this type of court. Then the judge calls for a break and we all file out of the courtroom.

In the lobby, the chief of security tells my brother that we can go and take pictures on the 13th floor if we like. We feel very privileged, as this doesn't happen very often. My brother reminds us that we cannot take pictures inside the Palace of Justice but when we get to the 13th floor our cameras go mad. We don't want to miss anything! When we leave we cross a peaceful and pretty park and go for a drink and talk about how happy we are to be here and see each other again. When it's time to go my heart is heavy as I don't know when I'll next see him. I turn to watch him walk away and pray that you will watch over him, Dad.

One more day and then we leave to spend the weekend with Dori. Before we leave we decide to go back to your resting place to spend a bit of time with you and place a small plant on your grave. It's a bit of an adventure as it's actually very difficult to find the exact spot in the park, even though Aida has given us the exact coordinates and a map! We have already attempted it once the previous evening as the cemetery was closing but ran out of time before we found you, so today we have to be right. I cannot fathom being in the area and not coming to see you.

Before we leave for Pennsylvania, Aida has called Uncle George and he has agreed to meet us. Marc and Dori are thrilled; I think it's important to them. When he arrives at the apartment I am a little overwhelmed, he is certainly an imposing figure! He looks at my sister and asks if I am Abie, then he squeezes my hand and steadily meets my eyes. I can't tell if he's looking for a resemblance with you, or some sign that yes, I am a Rivera. I observe this man who has known you so well and take in his bright smile, impressive build and incredible form for his age. We go and sit in the lounge where we exchange small talk for a while about tradition and customs in our country and his. Then he tells me about himself and about you and I don't dare ask any questions, I just let him remember at his own pace, his own time. My biggest fear is not understanding everything so I listen intensely and try not to miss a word. He cannot stay long as he is having an eye operation the next day. It was a wonderful moment but tinged with shyness and slight discomfort. Did he know I existed?

On the day we leave for Pennsylvania, I am happy but also sad to leave Aida. Before we go she takes me in her arms and tells me not to cry, because every time I arrive I laugh and every time we have to leave I cry. I tell her it's ok and hold back the tears with all my might. I can see in her face that despite her smile, she is suffering too. But she manages not to cry so I do the same. I love this woman, this mother, this friend.

Heading to Pocono! No problems finding *La Casita* this time around! Dori now lives here full time with her husband and children, which is great because otherwise Aida would have had to sell it. It's a bit far from New York for her now, but it would have been tragic for the family to never again see this place in the middle of the woods. I am especially pleased, as I desperately wanted Pascale and Daniel to have a chance to see it. They love it. Your office is no longer used as such and Dori has decorated to her taste, but it doesn't matter, the charm is still there. I show Pascale the glass cabinet containing all your memories and most treasured possessions and we are all once again impressed by the honour bestowed on you. Dori tells me she has kept all your photos and medals in boxes in the basement and we are welcome to take whatever we like. We go down to the basement feeling like kids on Christmas morning. She shows us three large plastic boxes full of treasure and we help ourselves to many framed pictures. Greg and I wonder how on earth we are going to travel back with them without them getting damaged on the plane. Dori also gives us two medals each and she gives me the flag that decorated your coffin. This is my most precious possession. You received the honours twice, once from the US Air Force and once from the New York Police Department, which is why you have two flags. What an honour for me to own one, I am so proud to bring back all these gifts and on the flight I didn't let the flag or the medals out of my sight I was so afraid that they would disappear at customs or that we would lose our luggage. I am taking a little piece of you home with me finally.

It's hard to go back to a routine after such an emotional journey, and we are still waiting for the results of the DNA test. Even so, I'm happy to go back to work and see my colleagues; it will help the wait go faster. The questions dance in my head non-stop: are you really my Dad? Did my mother lie to everyone and about everything? And if science tells me you are not my father, what will I do? I would feel embarrassed at having bothered your family for nothing! And I would be utterly crushed by the realisation that I'd got it all wrong. I am scared. I have to admit it. I am scared of the truth, but Pascale and I are ready to face it. We have to know. After all this time searching, the answer we are looking for is within reach, and it turns out just a phone call away.

On Friday, May 15th 2015, at 6:33pm, we receive an email from Aida who tells us she has received a call from the lab before the official results arrive by mail. The mystery will finally be broken. I can't believe that after all this time, the answer to all our questions and all our doubts is held within these three columns of digits on one piece of paper. I stare at them and think to myself that we are nothing in the scale of the universe,

just a few numbers that I can't understand. Beneath the numbers is a summary. The only part that really counts:
- Pascale: 0.24 meaning highly unlikely
- Abie: 96.5 meaning highly likely

I am elated! I finally have an answer. I can finally truly say without a shadow of a doubt that I am your daughter, and that I am Dori, Robert and Marcus' sister. Their blood, your blood, run through my veins and I have never felt more happy and relieved.

But at the same time, I am infinitely sad, disappointed and angry. I can't help but cry at the knowledge that Pascale's life is still built on a lie, that she is back to square one and will probably never know the truth about her history. She is now in the same situation as my sister Alexandra. It's very hard to imagine for anyone who hasn't lived it, just how difficult it is not knowing where you come from and who you are. It hurts in my bones and in my heart that my sister must continue to know that suffering. I must call her, but I'm anxious, as I know she must be heartbroken. I am already expecting what she says to me. She struggles to digest the information and all her anger and hatred towards our mother spills out over the phone. I completely understand. It's hard, she is suffering and she feels lost. I cry with her, the situation is unfair and I am angry too with our mother for all the lies she has told and all the pain she has caused. How will Pascale rebuild herself after this discovery? Especially as she knew you, she has photographs of herself in your arms and always thought they were the arms of her father... Why did our mother need to hide this information from us? She could have told us when we were teenagers or even when we were older, we asked so many questions! The truth would have been a weight off Pascale's chest, giving her hope that she may one day find her father, the same way it could have been for Alexandra who has lived with the same doubt her whole life.

After our first trip to New York I had written to my mother to tell her about our discovery and to beg her to speak to Pascale and Alexandra and finally give them some closure because my happiness was tainted by them not knowing. Sadly no reply came. I wasn't surprised, we haven't spoken for some years, but I still can't get over the fact that she would do that to her daughters. That she would deny them the chance to know their origins. I thought she would have some compassion, that she would try to remember or at least be honest and admit to not knowing, that she would at least try to do something, or say something, to make it easier for them. There's nothing worse than silence as a punishment from a parent, but why punish them? Why the silence? I think that with time she has reached a stage when nothing and no one can reach her. Her lies have become her truth. My heart crumbles like it did when we were kids and something happened to Pascale. Even though she was the eldest she has always been smaller than me and I always felt that I had to protect her. I couldn't bear to see her hurt.

But for me this doesn't change anything. She is and will always be my sister. And for our American family, things haven't changed either, as Aida put it so beautifully:

> *"Remember, family does not mean just blood relations. What counts is what is in our hearts for you and we all love you. You will always be a part of us and our family."*

The End.